The Cool Stuff Jar

Three Simple Ways to Live a Happier Life

Cass Mullane

© 2018 Cass Mullane. All Rights Reserved.

Limits of Liability and Disclaimer of Warranty

The author/publisher shall not be liable for your misuse of this material. This book is strictly for informational and educational purposes.

Warning – Disclaimer

The purpose of this book is to educate and entertain. It is distributed with the understanding that the publisher is not engaged in the dispensation of legal, psychological or any other professional advice. The content of each entry is the expression and opinion of its author and does not necessarily reflect the beliefs, practices or viewpoints of the publisher, its parent company or its affiliates. The publisher's choice to include any material within is not intended to express or imply any warranties or guarantees of any kind. The author and/or publisher do not guarantee that anyone following these techniques, suggestions, tips, ideas, or strategies will become successful. The author and/or publisher shall have neither liability nor responsibility to anyone with respect to any loss or damage caused, or alleged to be caused, directly or indirectly, by the information contained in this book.

ISBN 13: 978-1984137494
ISBN 10: 1984137492

THANK YOU

Robin McPeek for seeing the possibilities for this book sitting right there in my sketchbook.

Jon Khoury for his thoughtful manuscript review.

Donna Kozik and her crew for taking me from "What am I doing?" to "It's done!"

Dutch Bros Coffee for setting a great example.

Barry for 36 years of unwavering love and support.

Contents

It Started with a Sticky Note 7
   Create Your Cool Stuff Jar 11

Choose a Positive Mindset 15

Build Neural Pathways 19
   Connect the Dots 22
   Be a Great Explorer and Learner 24
   Widen the Gap 27
   Narrow the Gap..................... 32

Tame Your Mind Monkeys 41

Drop a Pebble in Your Pond........... 49
   Elect Yourself President of Your World .. 51
   Create a World That YOU Want to
   Play In 53
   Case In Point: Dutch Bros Coffee 55

Give Yourself Permission to Play....... 61
   It's OK to Play 65

Develop Your Sense of Play............ 66
Make It Fun 68
Add Play to Your Relationships......... 70
Competitive Play 72
Social Play 73
Add Play at Work 74
Add Play to the Corporate Culture 79

Cultivate Creativity 85
Let's Get It Back – Reinjecting
Creativity........................... 86

Join the Cool Stuff Jar Movement 95

It Started with a Sticky Note

It started with a sticky note.

Back when I was a shy, quiet introvert working in the corporate world, I was good at my job and responsible for some important projects and programs, but I rarely found the courage to stand up for myself. My current friends and colleagues would not recognize me because I'm much more outgoing these days. But that was how I started.

Then one day, one of my bosses gave me a memo about a project I'd been working on. On top of the memo he placed a yellow sticky note that said, "Nice job, Cass." It made me feel special because he'd taken the time to acknowledge me and to pat me on the back.

I wanted a reminder of that day, so I took the sticky note off the memo and stuck it in a little bowl in my desk drawer, way in the back. It was not my original intention to fill up the bowl, but as time went by, I regularly started jotting down onto slips of paper the good things that happened, and dropping those notes into the bowl.

About a year later, I changed offices. While clearing out my desk, I noticed the bowl overflowing with tiny little notes, so I dumped them all into an envelope and took the envelope home. That night, I read every single note. What had been a simple reminder of a job well done had become a collection of accomplishments at work that year, big and small.

Up until I saved the "nice job" sticky note, I hadn't kept track of my good work, or the results I generated for the company. I looked at the brightly colored mound of good and awesome things I'd learned, attempted, and accomplished that year and realized, "I should use this for my annual review."

So I gradually re-filled the bowl with all of the new cool stuff I did at work, and my confidence grew. Every time I glanced at the new stack of notes, surrounded by colorful lines you were given "Thumbs," you knew it meant you had truly earned peer and management recognition and respect. At the end of the quarter we held a party for employees who had earned Thumbs and gave out rewards varying from the nicer corporate logo items to significant cash bonuses. It was a particularly fun program because employees from the mailroom to management were participating. The corporate culture within the unit changed from run-of-the-mill to active and engaged. Members of the unit could not help but notice the cool stuff that was happening.

Through it all, I kept track of the good stuff I did—whether it was finishing a project ahead of schedule, solving a tough problem, learning a lesson from something that did not go perfectly or coming up with a new idea or strategy. I simply jotted each success down on a colored file card and dropped it into my Cool Stuff Jar. By doing that simple, *concrete* action, which reinforced my sense of value, I was able to break through a glass ceiling. It had taken so much work to get there, but I did it. I did it by discovering and acknowledging the innate power within me that initially only I was only able to see: the tangible evidence collected in my Cool Stuff Jar.

And all of it started with one little yellow sticky note.

Create Your Cool Stuff Jar

So what exactly is a Cool Stuff Jar? Well, it's really two things - one literal, one figurative:

1. A literal jar into which you drop in slips of paper that have the juicy cool stuff written down.

2. A state of being, a feeling or mindset that makes a point of focusing on and celebrating the good stuff that happens each and every day.

In this book, I will show you how to create a Cool Stuff Jar mindset, how to ensure that your Cool Stuff Jar mindset is sustained and how to ensure the amazing power of play and creativity are fully incorporated into your life. I will also challenge you to expand your Cool Stuff Jar attitude well beyond your own immediate world.

When you create your own Cool Stuff Jar, you'll take your first step toward changing your mindset and changing your world. Keep it simple. I suggest that you keep a small pad of paper that you like using right by your jar along with a couple of pens. That way, you have all you need to capture the cool stuff that happens every day. Try jotting things down in the morning, to begin your day on a positive note, again when you stop for lunch, and again, just before you leave to close your day. You might even set a digital reminder for the first week or so.

My own jar is about eight inches tall, and it's glass so I can see all the fun colorful slips of paper piling up. I make the slips by chopping up leftover art papers, scrapbook papers and colored file cards. I keep a pile of them along with a couple of fun pens right by my jar. The lid is simple to lift off and put back on, so it's easy to jot down cool stuff, date it and toss it in the jar without skipping a beat.

Let's get going!

CSJ Starter Slips

	Date
Create your Cool Stuff Jar!	
Help someone create their Cool Stuff Jar	
Give someone a Cool Stuff 'Starter' Jar	
Write down some of your innate skills	
Celebrate coming up with a good solution	

Use this as a checklist to get started, then as you complete these items, make sure you jot them down on a slips of paper and drop them in your Cool Stuff Jar.

Choose a Positive Mindset

"Whether you think you can or think you can't, you're right." – Henry Ford

Your mindset, or the way you approach living your life, is everything. It directly affects your happiness, your ability to cope, your relationships, and your well-being. Understanding how it works is important. From your internal self-talk to the way you respond to situations you find yourself in, your mindset will drive both your perceptions of a situation and which path you choose in response to each situation.

> **MINDSET:**
> A fixed mental attitude or disposition that pre-determines a person's responses to and interpretations of situations.

This is why having your own Cool Stuff Jar is so important. By making it a practice to find and to acknowledge the good things by adding them to your jar, you will begin shifting your mindset to a more positive and open place. Having a positive mindset is very powerful.

In order to train your mind to be more positive, you need to intentionally look for the good around you. Then, you simply need to write it down and drop it into your jar. The act of seeking, writing and dropping into the jar becomes habit. That habit shifts your mindset to a place where you are constantly appreciating the good that is going on around you. It becomes natural. And when that happens, you have created a new way to perceive and respond to your everyday situations that, previously, you may not have paid attention to.

Those perceptions and resulting actions of mindset follow a pathway—a neural pathway. There are literally millions of well-defined neural pathways in your brain. When a situation triggers your brain, you normally have a response that follows a pre-determined neural pathway and that path is ready to use at any given moment.

So let's see how neural pathways work, how to manage the gaps between when something triggers you and when you respond to the trigger. At the close of this chapter, I'll show you a fun way to manage your internal conversations.

and doodles, I felt strong and happy. Those positive feelings of being creative, innovative and valuable, stayed with me all day.

As, my mindset began to shift, I started to see myself in a different light. Keeping track of all of my success at work gave me the courage to say, "Hey, I am creative. I am innovative. I have a lot to offer," and to start going after projects I would not have gone after before. I earned respect from my peers and superiors for doing quality work, and with that came the promotions and greater responsibility. Eventually, I attracted the right people to my teams, and together we got amazing things done. Everyone functioned at the highest levels.

As a manager for a business unit at a financial services company, we were tasked with creating an employee rewards program. We called it Thumbs Up. Each employee was issued six Thumbs Up stickers per quarter and their mission was to find other employees in the unit who were going above and beyond in their jobs and to reward them with one of the Thumbs Up stickers. Since so few were handed out, the Thumbs Up stickers proved precious. When

Build Neural Pathways

In the delightfully complex system that is your brain, you need a path. Neural pathways are the road map that connects all parts of your brain. The more pathways you have the more alternate routes you have. Having

> **Neural Pathways:** The road map that connects all parts of your brain.

more alternate routes increases your ability to be more creative. This also means you can learn to quickly shift from one mode of thinking to another simply because your routes are varied and you know you can build a new path when you need to.

For example, when you decide to drive to the office supply store you have a normal route that you follow. When there is construction, you probably have another route or two. You could also skip the trip altogether and order online. The more routes you have, the more you enhance your ability to be creative in finding solutions. You don't have just Route 1 and Route 2, you also have Route Violet and Route Q.

Apply that same thinking to your neural pathways to travel from one area to another. The more routes you have to get from Point A to Point B, the better. That way when you encounter an obstacle or you need to come up with another route, you know that you have a myriad of choices available. This also means you can learn to quickly shift from one mode of thinking to another simply because your routes are varied and you know you can build a new path when you need to.

So, let's say you need to figure out how to better own your time when you are at work. You always seem to be under the gun, working late and rushing to finish many of your tasks. You then find yourself slipping into that messy, stressed out downward spiral that ends up with you barely able to function, much less keep up with work. Your well-traveled neural pathways here may follow this sequence:

1. I have way too much to do.

2. What's the most important thing to do?

3. All of them.

4. I think I'll call in sick tomorrow.

Rather than following the old neural pathways and checking out of work (which only creates more stress about the work still waiting for you at the office), let's try a new set of neural pathways, an alternate route:

1. I have way too much to do.

2. Is there anything I can delegate?

3. What can I take off my plate?

4. Which is the most important thing to get done right now?

5. What's the first step on the most important thing?

6. Ok, let's get to work and knock out the first step.

7. Woo Hoo! Nice job taking that first step!
8. Drop a slip in my Cool Stuff Jar.

> ## Cool Stuff Jar
> I took action by
>
> _____
> _____
> _____

I have found that taking action is a great way to keep your mindset healthy despite having what feels like a mountain of work to accomplish. When you break the perceived mountain into more manageable steps, and you then actually <u>take</u> a first step (however small),celebrate it. Then it becomes easier to move to the next step and the next. Building new neural pathways is the key.

Connect the Dots

How do you build a neural pathway? You simply connect the dots. Ask a question and answer it in a different way. You take an unfamiliar problem and you solve it. You feel a stimulus and you respond to it in a new way.

When you connect the same dots the same way over and over in your brain, you build reliable well-traveled paths. These paths are familiar, secure, effective, productive and comfortable. They may be direct routes or they may travel via a few locations.

Sometimes, a path can become a rut. It can get so deep that you lose sight of other options that exist. If it's a good rut, like always slowing down when you see the traffic light turn yellow, you probably want to keep that rut and travel it most of the time. If it's a bad rut, like always being angry and aggressive toward coworkers, you probably want to change it because you are suffering negative consequences from being in this rut. Either way, your brain is simply following a familiar path.

This is when having a large number of pathways to choose from can really be beneficial. When the path is a bad one, you need to learn to stop, step back and build a new neural pathway. By choosing to make another route you give that rut a chance to fill back in and to become just another option instead of a gully to fall into. You can open your mind to possibilities and make new choices.

Be a Great Explorer and Learner

You should know that you can build a new neural pathway any time you want to. Some of the best slips in my Cool Stuff Jar are about things I've learned. All you need to do is connect dots that are not currently connected. Sometimes you're also creating the dots, sometimes you're using existing dots. Either way, this is where the magic happens!

> **Creativity:** Mental characteristic that allows a person to think outside the box, which results in innovative or different approaches to a particular task.

Let's say you want to develop your creativity in order to open your mind to bigger and more innovative thinking. Perhaps you need to come up with a clever way to attract more clients or customers. Or you need to design a way to successfully manage a brand new fundraiser for your favorite nonprofit. Because both are big tasks you absolutely need to tap into your creativity to arrive at some viable options.

When you were a kid, your creativity was in full bloom, unfettered by the demands of life, society and expectations. So first, you need to go on an expedition to rediscover the old neural pathways you traveled when you were a kid. Once you find them, dust them off and start traveling them again.

Cool Stuff Jar
I learned _____

_____

_____ today!

Think of creativity as a muscle that you train. Once you've got it trained, you can automatically travel down any number of pathways. When you're ready, you will build new pathways and gain the confidence to not be deterred. How do you make this happen? By doing something unfamiliar. Take a crack at figuring out something that has been puzzling you. Sign up for a class, learn something new, walk somewhere you have not walked before.

Often what you need to do when you want to develop new neural pathways is simply to realize you're going down the same old path, stop, and switch to a new one. Connect the dots differently or explore something completely new to you. You will then have a more nimble mind. And a nimble mind is a powerful tool. Not to mention that it helps stave off some of the memory issues you may develop as you age.

Of course you need to make a conscious and intentional choice to do something new. You need to feel enough dissatisfaction with the same old routine that you want to make a change. Or, you need to feel that tickle of curiosity that makes you decide to go out and explore. You will find that a curious mind is a great thing. It helps you leap into your world filled with excitement and energy. It puts you in a good mood and you start anticipating each day as a new adventure.

One of my favorite questions that I teach clients to ask themselves is, "What if...?" What if you delegate the social media to someone who loves to do it? What if you develop an online program? What if you add a zero to your thinking and go for an extra $100,000? Try asking yourself, "What if...?" and let your mind open up to devouring the possibilities that spread out before you.

When you take the step to open up your thinking by asking "What if...?" you will likely see things that you had not seen before. For example, you will begin to consider what is possible instead of wasting energy on what is not. This is a great opportunity to add a slip to your Cool Stuff Jar acknowledging your newfound vision. And the more often you stop and take 10 seconds to grab a slip of paper, jot it down and drop it in the jar, the more quickly you will get those new neural pathways up and running.

Widen the Gap

An important aspect of changing your overall perspective on your world involves becoming acutely aware of how you interact with your environment and how you respond to the situations that come up and surprise you. What if you could take an extra couple of seconds before you respond and give your reply a more rational look? Creating that additional moment of time is the definition of widening the gap.

Your ability to control your knee-jerk reactions is critical to maintaining a calm, reasoned approach. Of course there are rare instances when you have only a nanosecond to respond, but what I'm talking about is the majority of situations that you'd encounter in your daily life.

Let's say you're in a meeting and that guy you think is annoying starts talking. You roll your eyes and in your head you tell him to hurry up and finish. You fidget, you sigh, you click your pen, you pull out your phone and check social media, you completely tune out. Eventually you get so frustrated that you might just pack up and leave the meeting.

The effect of your response is that you not only devalue his input, but you take your ability to reason out of the game, which immediately devalues you. What would happen if this time he said something important or even critical to the success of your group... and you did not hear him?

Keeping your head and thinking before you act is a great goal to strive for. After all, wouldn't you prefer to be considered a reasonable person over coming off as unreasonable? Think of the advantages: you're more likely to be heard, people are more willing to cooperate with you, your opinion is considered, your team wants to work with you, your peers respect you.

When you are unreasonable, what happens? People respond angrily, they shut down communication, they may go out of their way to undermine you, they don't want to be anywhere near you, and they sure don't want to cooperate with you or even work with you.

Think about a time when you had a knee-jerk reaction to a situation that you later regretted. We all have them, someone says something that pushed one of your buttons and you fire back a response that might not be well considered or appropriate. Then, either you decide you could care less or regret sets in. Either way, you pay the consequences.

When you're tuned in to your own hot buttons or pre-programmed responses to various stimuli, you give yourself a chance to recognize what's going on when a knee-jerk reaction starts. You then have the opportunity to spend that extra nanosecond considering an appropriate response before you blurt out something "stoopid."

So here are four suggestions to help you widen the gap:

1. **Breathe**. Physically take a slow, deep breath before you respond. You'll find that this immediately calms the knee-jerk response and gives you time to engage your brain and come up with something more considered.

2. **Become acutely aware of your hot buttons**. Recognize when they're being pushed and mentally take a step back before you deliver your reaction. Just the act of identifying that a hot button is being pushed puts some distance between the pushing and your response.

3. **Do something unexpected**. By this I mean choose something that is not what you

would normally do. For instance, when that annoying guy is saying things that have always put you on the defensive in the past, choose to say, "Let me think about your position for a while then I'll get back to you." This gives you time to calm down and respond more effectively instead of emotionally.

4. **Drop it and Zip it**. This is a trick that I learned in my early 30s. Drop your pen on the floor. As you reach down to pick it up, envision a giant zipper running from your feet to your head. Then, zip up the imaginary zipper as you bring yourself up to your upright position. (I sound like a flight attendant!) What this does is infuse you with a sense of alignment and strength. You will find that your energy is suddenly increased and your head is clearer. Give it a try.

Now that you know how to widen the gap between a situation occurring and your reaction, put it into action. You know a situation will occur that will test you. It could be driving to work or waiting in line or dealing with coworkers, family or friends. When it does, and you want to respond in the same old way, take the opportunity to make a different choice and widen the gap. And when you do, take a moment and celebrate your positive action by adding a slip to your Cool Stuff Jar. The more often you do this, the more quickly widening the gap will become more natural.

You do not need to widen the gap on every situation that arises because you already have a large number of perfectly appropriate responses available to you. Widening the gap is applicable when you need to develop better choices in responses to regular situations (like the guy who annoys you at meetings) and to create new responses to unexpected or extreme situations (like a crisis).

Narrow the Gap

Related to widening the gap is narrowing the gap. I know you've experienced the moments when you fall flat on your face. An example is when you produce something that you're proud of and it gets shot down. Or you forget to make a call and you miss an important meeting. Or you totally mess up and do a project completely wrong. You thought things would go one way, then they turn out to be the exact opposite and you're suddenly left gasping for air like you were punched in the gut.

You also know what it feels like to have someone say something hurtful about you. It could be criticism, meanness, gossip, or an intentionally condescending or demeaning statement. Whatever form it takes, it really hits you hard.

The result is that you get stopped dead in your tracks. You feel humiliated and embarrassed, your self-worth tanks and you just want to go off and be invisible until the mess blows over. You could be down for a few hours or that feeling could go on for months. Not good.

What's important is that you learn how to narrow the gap between when you go down and when you're back up and reengaged in your world. This is when having your own Cool Stuff Jar and establishing the quality habit of adding to it every day can help.

When you focus on the good stuff, you see more and more of it around you. It's as if all of a sudden cool stuff is popping up everywhere.

> **Law of Attraction:**
> Belief that by focusing on positive or negative thoughts a person brings positive or negative experiences into their lives.

It's the basic law of attraction in action. You can see it all around you and you're benefitting from shifting your focus squarely to the things you want more of. So the good just starts coming. Of course it was already there all around you, you just weren't ready to see and fully appreciate it.

In terms of narrowing the gap, when the crummy thing happens, you're certainly permitted to feel bad for a while, but you want to limit that time spent in the yucky place.

Here are four tips to narrow the gap:

1. **Read from your Cool Stuff Jar.** Stick your hand in your Cool Stuff Jar, pull out a few slips of goodness and read them. This will disengage your brain from its 'I'm-going-to-continue-to-spiral-down' neural pathway and place it on the 'I-feel-pretty-good-about-this' neural pathway. This simple act

of switching to a new thought pathway will help fill in the previously deep neural rut and create a new route for your thinking to follow that is more productive and narrows the gap between when you go down to when you resurface.

2. **Think about something you really enjoy.** When your mind is engaged in thinking about something you really enjoy, your whole body appreciates it and revels in the thoughts and associated sensations. For instance, I love the feel of cool crisp mountain air dancing on my skin and the sound of the breeze rustling the aspen leaves. Whenever I think of that sensation, I relax, breathe deeply and immediately move to a calmer place. When you think about things you enjoy, make sure to engage as many of your senses as you can. See it, touch it, smell it, taste it and hear it. You'll quickly start to feel the joy and happiness of doing something you love and you'll stimulate the pleasure centers in your brain.

3. **Write five things for your Cool Stuff Jar.** Grab five slips of paper and a favorite pen.

Think about what has happened today and jot down something cool on each of the five slips of paper and add today's date. Be fully present in the process and be mindful of the awesome things around you. Don't judge what pops into your mind, just capture it. Now, drop those five slips of happiness into your Cool Stuff Jar. As you write, more and more things will pop into your mind. (You're not limited to five slips of paper, by the way, feel free to keep going!) You will most likely find more than five things to celebrate. In fact, what often happens is your mind is flooded with cool stuff possibilities. Shifting your focus from the Yuck to the Yes can quickly reduce the painful moment to a mere trifle. The crummy thing still happened; acknowledge it, but then intentionally shift your attention back to the cool stuff again. The simple act of engaging your brain to pick out good things from the day will narrow the gap and bring you back to a better state more quickly. You get more of what you think about most. Choose more of the good stuff.

4. **Do something you really enjoy.** Instead of just thinking about it, get up, unplug and *do* something that makes you happy. Your body will respond, your emotions will respond, your mind will respond. There's nothing like doing the real thing to get you feeling good and back on track. As I mentioned earlier, I love the mountains. For me doing something I enjoy often means hopping in my car and heading up the pass to get a mountain fix. It does not take long and the benefits to my thinking are immense. I quickly shed the crummy stuff and revel in the magical place I live. That puts it all back in perspective for me. What is it that you love to do? Go do it.

Cool Stuff Jar
I responded well when _____
_____
_____

When you make a concerted effort to widen the gap and to narrow the gap in your responses you are building new neural pathways and alternate routes in your brain. The more you have, the easier it is to consciously and intentionally pick another route in order to move more quickly into a better place in your thinking.

When you get comfortable widening the gap and narrowing the gap between a stimulus and your reaction, you are beginning to make your world a Cool Stuff Jar world. You are intentionally choosing your response and making that response a more productive one. You are waving goodbye to knee-jerk reactions and reducing the time you spend in downward spirals. The effect on your world may be barely noticeable at first, but one day sooner or later you will wake up and realize how far you've come and how awesome your world—the world that you are creating—has become.

CSJ Starter Slips

	Date
Find six things to add to your Cool Stuff Jar right now	
Create a new neural pathway	
Write down an unexpected alternate route	
Acknowledge a lesson learned	
Jot down something new you learned today	
Do something you have not done before	
What made you curious today?	
"What if…"	
How did you widen the gap today?	
How did you narrow the gap today?	

	Date
Think about what you really enjoy	
Do what you really enjoy	

Use this as a checklist to get started, then as you complete these items, make sure you jot them down on a slips of paper and drop them in your Cool Stuff Jar.

Tame Your Mind Monkeys

So what happens when you're ready to try something new and that voice inside your head jumps in and immediately cuts you off?

It is essential that you pay attention to what goes on in your head. Do you spend most of your time thinking about the good stuff and filling yourself with positive and productive energy? Or do you regularly slip into negative thought ruts without even realizing it? Do you walk away when people start to gossip, or do you join in and then chew on it for hours in your mind? Do you focus on the good stuff that actually happened or do you often imagine the worst-case scenario?

If you are more the latter, and choose the worst-case scenario, let me assure you that you're not alone. Everyone has internal conversations going on all the time. These internal conversations are as varied as snowflakes and can encompass everything from deciding what shirt to wear with what pants, to wondering how big the universe really is. They can be fantastically positive and productive, they can be devastatingly negative, and they can be ambivalent, meandering wonderings. The thing to remember is that your mind only hears words. Your state of mind and your emotions determine the effect of your internal words. The trick is to be able to tune in and quickly dissipate the negative thinking and replace it with better thinking. So let's talk about mind monkeys.

When negative self-talk starts up in my mind, I picture monkeys swinging around from branch to branch inside my head chattering away. I call them "Mind Monkeys." Here's an example of what the voice might sound like in some of my clients:

Client: "Maybe I should enter a piece into this art show."

Mind Monkeys: "Ooooh, what makes you think you're good enough to enter that show? You don't exactly have a degree in Art-ology, do you?"

There is a specific way to deal with the Mind Monkeys and their negative, unproductive chatter. It consists of three simple steps.

1. ***Identify*** that they're starting in with the negative chatter.

2. ***Interrupt*** the chatter by throwing them a mental banana.

3. ***Replace*** the chatter with something better, something more positive and productive.

So, when my clients start hearing their internal Mind Monkeys launching into the negative, self-criticizing chatter about entering an art show (**Identify**), they know to hit the mental brakes and toss those monkeys a banana to chase (**Interrupt**), then swap that negative thought for a positive thought about entering the show (**Replace**).

Here's that conversation again:

Client: "Maybe I should enter a piece into this art show."

Mind Monkeys: "Ooooh, what makes you think you're good enough to enter that show? You don't exactly have a degree in Art-ology, do you?"

Client: "Here's a banana, go chase it. Whether or not I get in the show, it's something I want to do."

> **Reframing:**
> A way of viewing or experiencing events, ideas, concepts and emotions to find more positive alternatives.

This positive three-step process is a way of reframing, and it's a most effective way to begin to train your mind to function differently. Think of reframing as restating the thought with a better twist. Instead of saying what you're going to stop doing or what you're not going to do, say what you *are* going to do. Focus on positive action, then take that action. Let's look at an example.

For some reason, one of the most taboo subjects to talk about in our society (next to sex) is money. So, let's talk about money. How good are you at managing your money? If your first thought is something related to, "I'm terrible with money. I cannot even do a budget, much less stick to it," then this is for you.

Your Mind Monkeys are having a heyday swinging around inside your head, aren't they?

They're chattering away telling you how awful you are with money, how you'll never be good at understanding it and that you might as well just give up. Rather than let them get away with reinforcing all your stinkin' thinkin' around money, what if you could calm them down a bit or even get them to go stuff a banana in their faces and stop chattering all together?

Let's try an experiment. First, say this sentence out loud. "I'll never be good with money." Now, say it again, with feeling, like you really mean it. "I'll never be good with money!" Ok, now stop and check in with your body. Are your shoulders starting to slump? Is your energy draining? Is your stomach starting to knot up? Are you noticing increased stress? Probably.

Now, let's reframe that negative, self-critical thought and replace it with something better. Say this sentence out loud: "I can get better at managing my money." Now, one more time, say it like you really mean it: "I can get better at managing my money!" Check in with your body again. Are you sitting up straighter? Do you feel stronger? Is your energy filling back up? By reframing your thoughts, you have quieted your Mind Monkeys and you're in a proper mindset to begin taking positive action.

Here are a few more examples:

- "I'm going to stop wasting time"
  "I use my time more wisely"

- "I've always been a procrastinator"
  "I'm taking action on something important now"

- "I hate exercising"
  "I love the results of exercising"

- "I'm not creative"
  "Everyone's creative, including me"

Get the idea? Try taking something negative in your head and reframing it in a more positive, productive way right now.

Cool Stuff Jar

I knew I could _____

_____

_____ , so I did!

It's amazing how something as simple as reframing your thinking can have such a profound impact on your physiology. Imagine how good you'd feel if you made a routine of having these regular mind checks and improving how you think. It does take some practice and it does require you to pay attention and tune into what's happening in your head. I assure you that the time you invest on this is time very well spent.

BONUS:

I often give my clients a little Mind Monkey card to carry around. It's about the size of a business card and has a goofy monkey with a banana on it. The purpose is to remind them to pay attention to what's happening in their heads and to remember to reframe their unproductive negative thinking.

Would you like your very own Mind Monkey™ card to carry with you? Visit www.ProsperCreatively.com/MindMonkeyCard, I'll send you one you can download!

CSJ Starter Slips

	Date
Throw your Mind Monkeys a banana today	
Shift your perspective on something; note how it feels	
Write down a negative thought you reframed	

Use this as a checklist to get started, then as you complete these items, make sure you jot them down on a slips of paper and drop them in your Cool Stuff Jar.

Drop a Pebble in Your Pond

*"The best way to predict the future
is to create it."*
– Peter F. Drucker

In this chapter, I want you to imagine what it would be like to have your own Cool Stuff Jar world. A world where you and those around you are happier, stronger and more productive. A world where people love to coexist and love to contribute. A world where people respect one another and where they choose to come to play. I want you to imagine an AWESOME world!

When you choose to create your own Cool Stuff Jar world, you create a world that is pleasant and hopeful. And mind you, it is a choice. You can always choose to be unhappy, to be grumpy, to whine and to wallow. But why? What does that accomplish?

I want you to have the goal of taking actions that improve your world. And by improving your world, you'll naturally have the opportunity to enrich other people who come in contact with your world. You set an example of how wonderful daily life can be and that it's possible for anyone. You're the one in charge and you're the one who can make changes. You can be the one who makes the choices that make a difference.

For instance, I've found that my art studio is a place where people tend to drop in and visit. They always say that they feel relaxed and happy there. I'm pretty sure it's not because my art is the best art on the planet. I think it is because I've chosen to live a Cool Stuff Jar life and to create a Cool Stuff Jar world there.

Some of my core values include: work hard, play hard, be humble and be kind. I do my best to live these values and I believe this is reflected at my studio and in my life. Because I choose to be happy and pleasant, I'm attracting people who share those values, as well as those who crave more happiness and fun. I also choose to work hard and hold myself and others to high standards. I believe many other people also want to do good work and to hang out with others who share that goal. And, of course, I like to play. So at any given moment we could be howling with laughter or having an impromptu dance party, all of which makes my studio a comfortable place to be.

Of course, life is not always peaches and cream. We all have our struggles and our heartaches. The thing about creating a Cool Stuff Jar world is that you create a place where you can better handle the challenges and cope with the stressors that land squarely in your lap with or without warning. Grief and trauma may happen, but you must know that you have a safe, solid world that is set up to help you get through those events. And, if you desire, it is also set up to give a landing spot to others who are going through their own struggles. The choice is yours. Do something positive and uplifting.

Elect Yourself President of Your World

As I was writing this, the 2016 presidential election in the United States had concluded and there was a tremendous amount of divisiveness and fear. Rather than let yourself slip into the dark place that fear can take you, I encourage you to shine a light on that fear, think bigger and make good choices for yourself.

When an election happens in the United States the results are... the results. Some people win, others do not. That is how democracy works. What is important is how you choose to respond. Each day you get to choose how you're going to show up. You have the privilege of making a change in the one place where you always have a direct impact, your own world.

Here's a novel concept: choose to show up as President of Your World. Show up as the competent, hard-working, delightful rock star that you are. Now, doesn't that sound more appealing? Choose to go to work on the things you can directly control and have an impact on. Choose to pay attention to what's working in your world and what's good in your world. And go out and get more of that. Choose to make your world the best place to be.

What this all means is that you're being proactive and deciding how you want to live and how you want to show up in your business and in your life. And, you're not going to accept anything less.

It also means you're setting an example that others can follow. Be an adult, be a leader, be confident in yourself and your abilities. Go out and show others how your world is thriving:

- You're able to roll with the things thrown at you (widening the gap).

- You're able to work through obstacles or around them (narrowing the gap).

- You're in charge of you and you just happen to be the newly elected President of Your World (kicking those mind monkeys to the curb).

Create a World That YOU Want to Play In

You can use your influence in a strong, positive, forward-looking way. It's your present and future. With your new tools you can think and act on what you need to do in your world to improve it. And, you can think and act on what you can do to make your world inviting for others to engage in. Then, you can invite them to share that world. Say something positive and forward-thinking on social media. Do something unifying. Post something uplifting. Make your future spectacular.

Drop your pebble into your pond and make some positive ripples. Look at how you can do something great for your clients and customers, your family and friends, that may get them focusing on their cool stuff. You can choose to do cool stuff for your peeps whenever you want. Send them something encouraging. Let them know that you're there for them. Let them know that you're ready to serve.

Cool Stuff Jar
I did something nice for _____

_____

_____

Go out and be President of Your World and make your world an awesome place to be.

Case In Point: Dutch Bros Coffee

Dutch Bros Coffee is the country's largest privately held drive-thru coffee company, with over 260 locations in seven states and over 5,000 employees. Dutch Bros Coffee was founded in 1992 by Dane and Travis Boersma: brothers of Dutch descent.

I am fortunate to have a Dutch Bros Coffee drive thru one block from my studio. As soon as I pull into the line for the drive thru, a smiling person bounds over, says, "Hi Cass, having your doppio today with steamed cream?" and taps my order into a tablet. We comfortably chat for a minute, then they trot over to the next vehicle. As I pull up to the pickup window, there is always upbeat music playing and again I'm greeted with a smile and a "Hi Cass!" from everyone in the booth who knows me. They take my money, stamp my card and hand me my steaming drink. I leave feeling the love.

What I can always expect at Dutch Bros is a cheerful smile and a quick cup of great coffee. I get the joy of participating in their goodness because I choose to be a customer. Dutch Bros is a model of consistency at dropping a pebble in their pond and improving their world.

Here's what they say on their website (dutchbros.com/about-us):

> **Coffee is what we do, but it is not who we are.**
>
> *Here, at Dutch Bros we live by three main core values. One cannot be sacrificed for another.*
>
> *All must work together in order to provide the best experience possible.*
>
> *We may be a coffee company, but we are in the relationship business.*
>
> **Speed**
>
> *We get it, time travel isn't real...yet. So we move quickly, pour fast and serve with a sense of urgency to ensure that our customer's time is spent living life beyond our window.*
>
> **Quality**
>
> *We know our products and have mastered our craft. Perfecting each customer's*

drink, by hand, is the name of the game. We know the magic is in the details and strive to give our customers a remarkable product, each and every time they visit any of our stands.

Service

We are committed to providing the best experience and enjoy positively interacting with everyone we meet. We genuinely care about every customer we see and do our best to find solutions to any problem that might come our way.

I LOVE Dutch Bros Coffee!

Dutch Bros' vision is a beautiful example of a simple, concise, effective set of core values. Everyone who works at Dutch Bros lives them and the customers experience them consistently. I'll bet many of their customers share the same core values, which is why they choose to spend their money there in the first place.

Are you running a relationship business? Can you and everyone in the company name your top core values? Can your customers name them?

Dutch Bros' emphasis on relationships ensures a loyal customer base. In addition, Dutch Bros gives away lots of free coffee and donates over two million dollars annually to local communities and nonprofit organizations. This is one organization that understands how to drop a pebble in its pond and "spread the Dutch Luv."

CSJ Starter Slips

	Date
How did you take charge of your world today?	
What example did you set today?	
Adopt a Cool Stuff Jar attitude today	
How will you thrive in your world today?	
Elect yourself President of Your World today	
Invite someone to join you in your new world	

Use this as a checklist to get started, then as you complete these items, make sure you jot them down on a slips of paper and drop them in your Cool Stuff Jar.

Give Yourself Permission to Play

"We don't stop playing because we grow old; we grow old because we stop playing."
- George Bernard Shaw

"It is a happy talent to know how to play."
– Ralph Waldo Emerson

You may have been taught that hard work is an essential stepping stone to success in business and life. In fact, hard work became the minimum standard by which you measured yourself and anything less was wasting time. What if I told you that there is something as equally important as hard work and just as essential to your success? Because there is something... it's called play. And you are hereby granted Permission to Play.

> **Play:**
> Activity engaged in for enjoyment and recreation.

Kids know how important it is to cut loose and go into the world of play. It's totally natural. As an adult, it needs to be just as natural. Whether it's bowling or bungee, checkers or chess, doodling or dancing, puzzles or pixels, just let your fertile imagination run wild. Kids get it and let me tell you it's just as important for adults to get into play mode as well. It just feels good to play.

> **Cool Stuff Jar**
> I played _____
> _____
> _____ today

A friend of mine volunteers to crew on a hot air balloon for fun. She gets up at 4:30 in the morning to help prep the balloon. Donning her leather gloves and sturdy boots, she unpacks the basket and burner, then lays out the colorful "envelope" (the familiar balloon part).

She and a few other people hold tightly to the ropes as the envelope gets inflated with helium and stands up. When the ropes start to strain to keep the balloon on the ground, they all pile into the creaking wicker basket and lift off. As they rise, it's delightfully peaceful and silent except when the hot burner blasts helium into the envelope. Her mind opens and the worries of the world shrink away as she gains altitude. She can see forever while she drifts with the winds and she expresses her joy and gratitude to the sky.

Play is essential for adults. It is an important source of stress relief and relaxation. It is also a great source of physical, mental and emotional stimulation in a fun, good, endorphin-releasing way.

These days we focus so heavily on the obligations of work and family and everything else that we think there's rarely room to squeeze in time for healthy play. So when we do get a chance for some down time, we're likely to veg out in front of the TV or computer instead of picking up something else to do like we did as kids. Just because you're an adult doesn't mean you cannot benefit from some fun, healthy, rejuvenating play.

Why did you stop playing in the first place? Maybe someone told you that playing was childish. Maybe you feel self-conscious, even inhibited. Maybe you feel a little embarrassed or silly. Perhaps you think that you have to be serious all the time in order to be taken seriously. Well, here's a new mindset to try on: So what?

There is a difference between being childish (silly and immature) and child-like (having good qualities associated with a child). Wouldn't you agree that kids are incredibly curious, inventive, astute, open-minded, creative and constantly learning? I think those are pretty substantial qualities for any adult. Wouldn't you want to exhibit those traits? I'd certainly consider those attributes as positive ones and make sure that I played regularly to keep them honed and thriving in me.

Play is particularly useful when you are faced with difficult situations. Smiling and laughter make you feel good. The good endorphins are released into your body. That good feeling sticks around even after the laughter subsides. Taking time to play or laugh can go a long way toward helping you feel better and maintaining a positive outlook.

Injecting play into your life has a mountain of benefits. Here are a few:

- Relieve stress and increase good endorphins
- Improve your brain function
- Boost your creativity and imagination
- Increase your ability to learn and solve problems
- Improve relationships and your connection to others
- Ward off stress and depression
- Keep you feeling young and energetic

It's OK to Play

Think back to when you were a kid. You were able to create your own games that did not involve anything other than a couple of sticks and your imagination. It was pure and simple.

It was engaging and it was stimulating. Most importantly, it was completely natural. Somewhere between then and now, you may have buried the joy that lies in play. It's high time to find it again. Being an adult does not exclude play from your life. It is just as important now as it was then.

Many of us make our life all about work and we forget that play is an integral component to living a full, well-rounded life. It's never too late to bring back your sense of play. Your age is irrelevant. A youthful state of mind is not only healthy as we age, it's just plain fun! If you have kids or grandkids, engage with them. If you have a pet, play with your pet. If you're flying solo, make sure you're doing something you enjoy every single week. Play needs to become part of your normal routine.

Develop Your Sense of Play

It was the idea of play that caused me to create my first Cool Stuff Jar. I worked in a cubicle early in my career and was not allowed to put anything on those dull gray scratchy fabric cube walls. So, I decided to put something more playful on my file cabinet. I added a colorful open mouth jar and made a game of wadding up paper and tossing it into the jar by banking it off the blah gray cube walls. Then the blah cube walls became fun. Eventually, that jar became my first real Cool Stuff Jar.

One of the best ways to develop your sense of play is to set aside regular time for quality play. Just like anything, the more you do it, the better you get at it. Don't worry about what other people think. You're trying to take care of yourself and get on a better keel. They probably could benefit from a little play, but it's your turn now. Remember, you need to put on your oxygen mask first before you can help anyone else, right? So go ahead. Laugh, smile, be spontaneous, joke around and play.

You don't need anything special to reintroduce play into your world, so here's how to get started:

1. Clear your calendar for a few hours.
2. Turn off all your electronics (like your phone, TV, computer... yes, you can do this).

3. Give yourself permission to do whatever you want to do for that block of time.
4. Go out and DO it.
5. Pay attention to how good you feel when you're done.
6. Repeat steps 1–5 regularly.

BONUS: Do this with another person or two and you'll increase the overall benefits of your play. Plus, your friends will benefit as well.

Make It Fun

Here are six ways to create opportunities to play:

- **Surround yourself with playful people.** Playful people are more likely to support your intention to play and to join in. They tend to be relaxed and easy to be around. They will help you plan fun activities and help you learn how to be more spontaneous.

- **Attend a regular evening out** with friends or family. Getting together with a group to socialize while doing something fun is a great way to connect and engage with others.

- **Set up time with colleagues from work** to go do something like miniature golf, bowling, karaoke or just taking a walk. Again, socializing outside of work creates deeper bonds.

- **Play with your pet** or borrow one if you don't have one. The simple act of petting a cat or a dog is known to reduce blood pressure. Imagine how good you'll feel after you play with a critter for a while.

- **Play with kids** and you'll get to really see the world through a kid's eyes again. Pay attention, let loose and goof around.

- **Create something new** with your friends using found objects, art supplies, or cool science kits. Your mind will be relaxed and open after this activity.

Cool Stuff Jar

I turned _____

_____

_____ into fun!

Add Play to Your Relationships

Playful encounters are often the most enjoyable for both parties. Whether it's romantic, work, an acquaintance like the cashier at the grocery store, pets, or kids, playful encounters tend to put everyone at ease. You smile and the relaxed feeling of well-being flows over you. Play induces that. It's like doing something good for someone else for no reason, that same yummy warm feeling.

Play is an effective tool for your relationship toolbox. It helps relationships feel fresh and exciting. When you inject play with others you're also injecting joy, relaxation and resilience into your relationships. You learn to trust one another, whether at work, romantically or with your family and friends. Your social skills improve, you learn cooperation and compromise. You establish a feeling of safety that enables you to try new things and think new ways.

A great example of play in relationships is flirting. It's an effective tool for attracting someone and for getting over the initial awkwardness that can happen when you're getting to know someone. In longer term relationships, play keeps things vibrant and continues to deepen intimacy and trust. It supports a strong foundation that helps you work through the disagreements that crop up over time. It is an essential component that brings people closer together by creating a positive bond. Think about how great you feel after you've done something playful. You're probably smiling, you're relaxed, you're breathing fully and you have a sense of satisfaction that you've done something good for yourself.

All of us need to play. It's part of our makeup to have chunks of down time that are spent in activities we truly enjoy. Whether we do it alone or with others, we require play to counter the effects of our crazy, over-scheduled, work-focused society.

When you play, clear your mind of work or other obligations and focus on the experience of play. Be fully present and in the moment. There does not need to be a point to play, no goals or hidden agendas. Just goofing around by yourself or with your friends, coworkers or family is enough. Simply have fun and enjoy yourself.

Competitive Play

Some of you thrive on competition when you play. It may be going all out for the win or simply enjoying the camaraderie of playing with others. This applies whether you're playing sports or playing cards. Organized leagues with varying levels of competition abound. So do groups that simply get together socially. All you need to do is find the one that's right for you.

For example, I used to be a competitive softball player. I was good enough that I was recruited to play in super competitive leagues. One league I played in lasted only one season. While I love playing competitive ball, I did not like the cutthroat level of performance that was expected in this league. I drew the line when I was told to slide in spikes up to break up plays at second and third. It goes against my fundamental value of never intentionally causing harm to another player. I shifted to another league that was also super competitive, but not so cutthroat. It suited my sensibilities better and I was much happier playing hard with that team. I enjoy winning, but what I enjoy the most is simply getting out there and playing.

Nowadays, I play for fun on a very non-competitive team from the building where I have my business. It's so non-competitive that we've only had one game... against ourselves! The whole idea is to get out on a Saturday morning and play with friends, then carry on with our day. We all leave practice feeling relaxed and refreshed. It's a great way to start the day and socialize outside of work. Plus, it builds a deeper bond among us at work.

Social Play

For others, competition has very negative associations. If that's the case with you, then forget about competition. Find non-competitive or social groups to join and make a point of engaging in play. Do whatever relieves your stress and what makes you happy.

I grew up in a family that really liked playing board games and word games. We routinely pulled out the games as soon as the table was cleared and the dishes were done. Everyone was engaged at whatever level they were comfortable. We learned how to play well, fairly and respectfully. These lessons translated to our careers and family lives. This routine also became something we kids carried forward into adulthood and we still enjoy playing games whether online or in person.

What if you hate playing games? Then don't play games! Play does not have to be structured. You can insert play into most any activity. Try taking yourself to the park and planting yourself in the grass under a shady tree to read a book, or taking two words and creating a brand new one, or adding the occasional skip into your walk to work. Go out and find something else that you like to do that makes you feel playful and relaxed, then go do that.

Add Play at Work

Think of your "good" bosses you have worked under. I bet that a sense of play was part of their personality. This does not necessarily mean they went around the office wearing a red clown nose and giant shoes every day, but it does mean that they knew when to relax and when to inject something playful into the work day. They also knew to encourage an appropriate sense of play in their team. For you, as the employee, that meant being at work was more pleasurable, it was somewhere you enjoyed going and the people were easier to be around.

I've worked on some great teams in my career. The sense of play fueled our problem-solving abilities, it fueled our imaginations and our creativity, and it led to innovation and a positive sense of self-worth. It fed our brains and strengthened our cognitive abilities as well as our respect for one another as we were free to explore and consider previously un-thought-of possibilities.

Many successful organizations recognize the value of play and can directly link working in a fun environment with innovation, increased productivity and a happier workforce. Art, games, exercise and meditation can be included as part of an employee's day and goes a long way in encouraging staff to let off steam and to relax. In addition, organizations often set up areas with comfortable, playful furniture for meetings or breaks. When employees do go back to their workspaces, they are returning with a fresh, open mind, ready to solve the challenges awaiting them. They also tend to have higher job satisfaction, better morale and, ultimately, they stay with companies longer.

Take the opportunity as often as possible to make what you're doing fun. Whenever you face a task that isn't particularly pleasant, try to think of a way to make it fun. For example, business owners need to create and maintain a business plan. Often this process is arduous and looked upon with dread by the team that needs to prepare the plan. The reasons are varied: you already have a full work load and now have to work this in... you know it will take hours of boring research... you know it will require contact with people you might not particularly like dealing with... you know it will be lots of late nights... you know management will tear it apart... and on and on and on.

Why not make that process fun? Make it colorful, make it something done at a fun location, when a section is complete, have a reward. Whatever it is, try to inject some fun.

I know someone who has made business plans fun for creative entrepreneurs. Her name is Jennifer Lee and she wrote *The Right-Brained Business Plan*. In it she walks through a way to create a business plan that wraps a lot of play in the actual work. The "playsheets" are colorful and inviting, the activities involve more than just crusty numbers and analytics, and the result is a vibrant, visual business plan. It is perfectly geared toward the needs of right-brainers and creatives, many of whom feel like their heads would explode if they had to build a standard business plan. In fact, her business plan is so fun that you'll actually use it instead of just leaving it on a shelf gathering dust.

My own business plan is an accordion book made from an old Bisquick box and poster board. I've also got a twisted spiral book that I use for regular updates. The cool thing about my business plans is that I use them regularly because they are playful and visually stimulating. When I complete something that was in my plan, I simply replace the old image with a new one representing the new goal. Because I actively use these plans, I am able to articulate every section of my plan. Try doing that with a dusty notebook full of charts and graphs that you haven't looked at in months or even years. Make it fun and you're more likely to fully engage with it.

As an employee, your success at work does not always equate with the number of hours you spend at the office; it often depends on the quality of your work. And the quality of your work is directly influenced by your sense of contentment and well-being.

> ## Cool Stuff Jar
> I filled my well by _____
> _____
> _____

When you take time to recharge yourself through play, it can be a great boost for your career. When you run into serious problems on a project, sometimes it's important to take a time out for play either by yourself or with your team. This does a lot more than just take your mind off the problem. When you play, you engage the creative side of your brain, leaving the logical side to wrestle with the problem without restraints. Often this gives you a chance to see things in a new light and to come up with an innovative solution.

Add Play to the Corporate Culture

What if you're in a place where play is not part of the culture? You can still inject play into your workday. Make a point of taking a creative break whenever you can. When you have lunch you could make it a game to look around your workplace and see if you can find the letters of the alphabet in your surroundings. Then snap a picture on your phone. For example, if you have a window with panes, you'll find the letter "E." The pattern on a carpet or a chair or a floor could yield several letters. Get the idea? Involve others in the hunt and you can build a playful bond with your coworkers.

Another great way to add to the fun is to create a Cool Stuff Jar for the team. Place it in an easily accessible area with plenty of papers and pens available for people to stop by and jot down something cool and drop it in the jar. Watching the papers pile up is a great indicator that the team is happy and functioning well.

When you add play at work you reduce your burnout and increase your engagement. You re-energize your mind and your body. You see problems in a new light and that helps trigger creativity, which leads to innovation. And when that increased stress arrives, you're better equipped to handle it.

From the boss' perspective, there is ever-increasing pressure to get more done with fewer resources. You need to juggle less money and fewer people to do the work, and you have less time to get it all done. You cannot continue to ask people to work harder and longer without having to deal with the consequences of chronic stress, more sick days, lower productivity, increased burnout and higher turnover.

A solution could be adding some time for recreation to keep employees more content. The workplace can be more light-hearted and employees can be encouraged to tap into their creative sides to conceive innovative solutions to problems. Encourage employees to get up and take breaks from where they are working and go to a place where they can take a breather and do something playful for a few minutes. Occasionally, you can toss in a few group activities like a mini-golf tournament or an office treasure hunt just to relieve stress.

Consider leaving crayons or Play-Doh® in the conference room. Just smelling those two items can take you back to childhood and put your mind into a more open, creative state. Or have a jigsaw puzzle in the break room where people can take a moment to use another part of their brain, then return to work refreshed. Remember, people who are feeling happy tend to be more engaged and are, overall, more productive.

When you work hard you need play to maintain a healthy balance in your life. Whether competitive, social or unstructured, play is essential. It can be as simple as shooting hoops against the garage or making up words. Plus, when you play with others, you build relationships and strengthen already established bonds. It relaxes you and engages you in a mindful way. You are hereby granted permission to play.

Bonus:

Would you like a fun visual reminder to add play back into your life? Or, better yet, how about a formally issued authorization to engage in playful activities that is valid across all international and interplanetary borders?

Visit www.ProsperCreatively.com/PermissionToPlay and I'll send you a permission slip you can download!

CSJ Starter Slips

	Date
I cut loose like a kid today when _____	
I felt those good endorphins today when _____ _____	
I enjoyed the feeling of playfulness by _____	
I added play at work today when _____	
I adopted a playful attitude today when _____ _____	
I felt recharged today when I _____	

Use this as a checklist to get started, then as you complete these items, make sure you jot them down on a slips of paper and drop them in your Cool Stuff Jar.

Cultivate Creativity

I think the number one thing people say when I suggest that they add creativity back into their world is, "I'm not creative." It always makes me a little sad when someone says that. The problem is that people think being creative means being artistic. The two are not the same.

Being an artist is just one incarnation of creativity. Another incarnation of creativity is a CEO trying to remain relevant in an ever-changing business environment. Other incarnations are a research scientist or an interior designer or a child trying to solve a riddle. Each needs to be creative in order to be successful.

Creativity takes many, many forms and shows up in practically all aspects of life. A number of the slips that end up in my Cool Stuff Jar relate to how I try to solve something particularly challenging. I happen to think that most everyone is creative because most everyone can solve problems. And problem solving requires you to think outside the normal box.

Being more creative starts with a mindset shift. You must embrace the idea that creativity is so much larger than being an artist. You must accept that while you may have temporarily subdued your creativity, you are a creative being. Once you make the shift, your world starts to sparkle.

Let's Get It Back – Reinjecting Creativity

If you allow yourself to think about it, you might feel that there's a hole inside where your creativity used to be and you're sad that it's gone. You miss the flow, the exhilaration, the relaxation and the mindfulness of being creative. In fact, without a dose of creativity, you might find yourself feeling stressed and grumpy. It's natural—being creative is part of what makes us feel like soulfull humans and not like a soul-less machine.

So let's take a quick look at why creativity may have been put on your back burner.

1. **Feeling guilty**. When you're being creative, the logical part of your brain may be thinking that it's not important or that it's a waste of time. Nothing could be further from the truth. It can be just as important as reviewing social media analytics or crunching some numbers. You need to do it to stay on top of your game and to stay sharp and nimble.

2. **Not easy to do**. This is you telling yourself a story. Remember that you're not creating an artistic masterpiece, you're simply tapping into what relaxes you and opens your mind. How hard is it to doodle or color in the boxes on a piece of graph paper to open your mind?

3. **Feel like it's stupid**. Feeling that creativity is stupid or childish is a mistaken belief many people have. In fact, creativity is not childish, it is more child-like, which is a good thing. Think about the smell of a crayon—it takes you back to a simpler, freer time, and will likely cause you to relax and reflect. This is being child-like, and this state of innocence and wonder is something that you want to become familiar with. It is in this state that your mind is open to exploring possibilities.

4. **It takes too much time**. What's the value of opening your mind up and immediately reducing your stress? Take 10 minutes for a quick creativity break (like solving a puzzle or walking around looking for the letter "K"). It doesn't take a lot of time to be creative and it's time well spent.

5. **Judgment by others**. The thing about judgment is that it's someone else's view, not yours. You don't have to buy into it. Your happiness should not be contingent upon someone else's approval. Ask for support instead of judgment. If you don't receive it, you may have to jettison those naysayers.

6. **I'm a perfectionist**. Maybe you tend toward the perfectionist side, and feel that if you're not going to be the next Einstein or Picasso, you're not going to do it at all. Let me stop you right there. When being creative (and doing a lot of other things in life) you want to adopt the attitude, "Good is good enough." Don't expect perfection out of the gate. After all, it takes decades, even lifetimes, for scientists and artists to master their craft. Why would you expect yourself to create perfection on your first try?

7. **I don't have creative supplies**. The same holds true with your tools and materials. You don't have to have the perfect tools or materials before you can be creative. Use what's available. Have plenty of paper, pens and a box of collected interesting stuff on hand so you can pick it up at a moment's notice and get creative.

You may be thinking this is all well and good, but how can creativity help me in my life? Glad you asked. Remember that creativity is that mental characteristic that allows a person to think outside the box and results in innovative or different approaches to a particular task. These days companies are specifically hiring out-of-the-box thinkers, innovators and creatives to add to their existing teams. They are looking for a fresh approach to their businesses and a fresh approach to resolving the issues that they face. They want to shake up the old paradigms and create a new way of doing business.

Here are five reasons to have a more creative workforce:

1. **Stress reducer**. Dealing with ever-changing, ever-growing responsibilities can lead to a mind-numbing existence at work. This, of

course, can lead to you being stressed out and unproductive. When you let creativity back into your life, even a few minutes at a time, you'll find yourself calmer, more relaxed and better equipped mentally to keep all your plates spinning. In addition, your blood pressure will go down and your ability to reduce knee-jerk reactions will improve, both of which reduce your overall stress levels.

2. **Open your mind to possibility.** If you live in a black and white world, you see all problems in black and white. But what if an answer you're looking for is chartreuse or royal blue? Being creative opens your mind and makes it more conducive to problem solving. It also gives you an opportunity to consider and explore ideas that might not show up in a strictly black and white world.

3. **Think vs. Feel.** Those who rely exclusively on analytical thinking may be tuning out subtle internal messages, like gut feelings. Being able to hear that internal conversation adds a new dimension to work life and can lead to better communication and understanding among people at your place of business.

4. **Competence and Confidence.** You've got to have competence to succeed, and having

competence will likely boost your confidence, which is also essential. It's important to feed both your competence and confidence. Recognizing your wins, even the small ones, helps you bounce back when you encounter obstacles. Fill your Cool Stuff Jar with those wins and celebrate your achievements and lessons learned!

5. **Make everything more fun.** Face it, you can use a little more fun in life. This doesn't mean you have to become a full-time circus clown or decide to chuck it all and take a stand-up routine on the road. But if you relax a little here, and allow the creativity in, you'll find life will respond and give you more reasons to smile and laugh. Isn't that what it's all about?

Cool Stuff Jar
I tapped into my creativity by _____
_____
_____

Don't let anything get in the way of tapping into your creativity. The point is not to eliminate your analytical thinking, but to give a chance, by looking inward, to give the high-performing analytical part room to breathe.

For instance, when studying for my MBA, I took both Micro and Macro Economics classes. While I understood the words and pretty much understood the concepts, it really wasn't coming to life for me. I got myself a set of highlighters and started coloring in the graphs and—lo and behold—it all came together. For me, color was the key that unlocked the door and made it real for me. It made me realize that I was smart in a different way—creativity helped me find that way. I want you to find your way.

Next, expand your thinking and imagine what it would be like if the people you hang out with most were doing the same thing. Imagine how powerful a handful of people intentionally choosing to work on changing their mindsets can be. Imagine how happy, productive, creative and innovative you can be. Imagine the impact on your home, your work, your community. Yep, imagine the pebble dropping into your pond and that wonderful ripple effect. That's the more expansive effect of the Cool Stuff Jar, which we're going to dive into next!

CSJ Starter Slips

	Date
I added creativity today when _____ _____	
I reframed my thinking about being creative by _____	
I merged business and creativity by_____	
I thought creatively today when _____	
I felt creative today when _____ _____	

Use this as a checklist to get started, then as you complete these items, make sure you jot them down on a slips of paper and drop them in your Cool Stuff Jar.

Join the Cool Stuff Jar Movement

As you build your Cool Stuff Jar routine, pay attention to how your outlook changes. Notice how you feel, what your thoughts are and how you interact with the people you come in contact with. Notice how even the smallest things have an elevated value. There's probably more good stuff happening around you than you ever noticed. Just because you hadn't seen it, doesn't mean it wasn't there. What it means is that you've successfully shifted your mindset and you can more fully appreciate and celebrate the great world you're living in.

And all this is happening just from putting a slip of paper in a jar.

Imagine what happens when you join the Cool Stuff Jar movement:

- Your stress levels drop and your joy and happiness go through the roof.

- You remain calm amidst chaos and move toward sustaining that sense of calm as your more natural state.

- You revel in a new ability to choose your responses and the positive effect this has on your strength and confidence.

- You make play and creativity part of your everyday routine.

- You learn to celebrate even the small things.

- You know what it feels like to be continually smiling, not just on the outside, but also on the inside.

Pretty awesome, isn't it?

Now let's go bigger. Ponder the effect your magical Cool Stuff Jar world will have on the people around you. They'll note your happiness and wonder what you're doing that's different. They may not even realize it consciously, but subconsciously they will feel the pull toward your world because they crave what you have.

Consider what it would be like to have the people around you creating their own Cool Stuff Jars and learning how to capture that powerful mindset for themselves. Think about what happens when you share this way of approaching life with them and the positive effect it can have on them. Think about how a simple shift in attitude can have a profound effect on someone else's world.

Finally, go even bigger and move beyond your circle of colleagues, family and friends. Imagine this thinking finding its way into *their* circles of colleagues, families and friends. Imagine it becoming a movement that goes global. It's an amazing feeling, isn't it?

So here's my challenge to you:

1. **Go out and create your Cool Stuff Jar.** Better yet, do it with a friend or two so you can hold each other accountable and get the good habit ingrained. (E-mail me a picture of your jar so I can celebrate with you! [CSJPics@prospercreatively.com]

2. **Expand your thinking to create your own Cool Stuff Jar world.** When your new Cool-Stuff-Jar-filling habit is firmly in place, and you've experienced that gentle yet powerful mindset shift, you can elect yourself President and create your new world.

3. **Share how you did it with others and spread the Cool Stuff Jar love.** When you're

comfortable, relaxed and confident, invite others to join you in this new way of living.

What are you waiting for? Create your Cool Stuff Jar movement!

CSJ Starter Slips

	Date
Create your first Cool Stuff Jar today!	
Help someone create their Cool Stuff Jar	
Give someone a Cool Stuff 'Starter' Jar	
Send a picture of your Cool Stuff Jar to Cass	
I elected myself President of My World today	
I shared my Cool Stuff Jar attitude with _____	

Use this as a checklist to get started, then as you complete these items, make sure you jot them down on a slips of paper and drop them in your Cool Stuff Jar.

CSJ Starter Prompts

Miscellaneous Ideas

	Date
Enjoyed a great cup of _____ today	
Made all green lights going to work today	
Made _____ really happy by doing _____	
Complimented _____ by saying _____	
I am thankful for_____	
Attained my goal of_____	
Made room on my plate for _____	
Added ____ new things to my Cool Stuff Jar today!	
I did a good job at _____ today	
Helped _____ stay accountable for_____	

	Date
Stayed on task with_____	
Made a realistic plan for_____	
Paid attention to my spending by_____	
Generated new revenue from_____	
I had the best lunch today	
Dropped something that wasn't serving me off my plate	
I ROCK!!!!!	
I am beautiful, inside and out	
It's 10:27… I know where my money is!	
I love my life	
I love being me!	
I love that I get to do my favorite things every day	
I OWN this	

	Date
I'm really good at _____	
I took a walk today	
I saw a [animal/bird/sea creature] today	
I felt strong like a _____ today	
I am strong	
I am flexible	
I am patient	
I am supportive	
I am Awesome!	
I am an amazing _____	
I'm really good at _____	
I am creative	
I'm a ROCKSTAR!	
My favorite superpower is_____	
I am a great person	

	Date
I feel great in my skin	
I am kind	
I am generous	
I am thoughtful	
I am delightful	
I know my stuff!	
I made my goal:_____	
This week was awesome!	
I am worthy	
I am happy	
I am a great friend	
I am a great coach	
I am a great partner	
I am a great parent	
I am a great spouse	

www.ingramcontent.com/pod-product-compliance
Lightning Source LLC
Chambersburg PA
CBHW071010080526
44587CB00015B/2418